Domesticated

Vol.2

More Words, Pictures, and Stuff.

James Domestic

Published by Earth Island Books
Pickforde Lodge
Pickforde Lane
Ticehurst
East Sussex
TN5 7BN

www.earthislandbooks.com

Copyright © 2023 James Domestic
First published by Earth Island Books 2023
Cover design by James Domestic

Illustrations and photo edits by James Domestic. Original photos credited.
Front cover photo by Mark Richards.

ISBN 9781916864009

Printed and bound by Solopress, Southend

For Lu, Freddie, and Suze –
Three cool cats*

*even though one is a human woman

Preface

I'm writing this preface at the arse-end of July 2023; a July that feels like the greyest, most overcast, damp, and downright shitty July I can recall. It's not especially cold, just drab and muggy. Unpleasant. Not summer. I'm starting to think, what with the way the weather's been going, that Seasonal Affective Disorder should get a brand refresh that includes a new moniker; nothing to do with the seasons themselves, because they're all screwed now aren't they? Global warming and all that shizz. Sheesh. So maybe we can call it Weather Affective Noggin Killer (W.A.N.K.), 'cos that's what it does at its worst; flings you into a pit of depression and anxiety that – if the seasons still did what they're *supposed* to do – doesn't lift until around March. If I could hibernate for four to five months a year, I would. No joke.

But things ain't that bad right now, and I'm usually able to temporarily lighten my mood somewhat by messing around with words if I can drag up the mental energy, so I'm lucky. Even luckier to have a publisher willing to put their faith in those words and turn them into the finished product you hold in your hands (or are perhaps reading on a tablet. Not a stone one; y'know, a Kindle or whatever. You ain't Moses).

This book – Vol.2 – is the filling of the 'Domesticated' sarnie. I've always envisioned this as a three part series of books, and work is already underway on the top slice of warm, heavily buttered crusty (punk) bread that'll finish the set.

James Domestic 20/07/2023.

Contents

Renewal

The very first daffodil of the spring
and the return of the housemartin
when butterflies appear by the pound
and summer's parcel is unbound

A roe deer's delicate form in a field
beer garden chatter; that holiday feel
signs of renewal, and a mental refresh
the first fart in a clean bed

The Mark E. Smith Curmudgeon Bible

She kept it in a carrier bag
for when the time was right
she'd give the tome some oxygen
and set the place alight
upon its many hallowed pages
caustic words that carry might
don't you know there's nothing that can rival
the Mark E. Smith Curmudgeon Bible

Inside: irascible instructions
courses in conversation contra
Can cassettes and Embassy
a dozen Holten stirs the monster
she, as if possessed by Smith
summons Muzorewi's daughter
you can make yourself vulnerable to potential libel
with the Mark E. Smith Curmudgeon Bible

Lagered lashings for the crew
rule with fear and rancour
tweak the tone of all they do

make them walk the plank-ah!
in the margin on page two:
"all musicians are wankers"
keep your mouth shut as the best means of survival
from the wrathful Mark E. Smith Curmudgeon Bible

All the text glows a fiery red
and pre-cog's now in tune
the lady knows instinctively
just what she has to do
bombast coursing through the veins
it's time to turn the screw
and Jesus is a bloke with loads of rockabilly vinyl
in the Mark E. Smith Curmudgeon Bible

Another bottle, and some speed
invective primed for baiting
page eights says "vituperation:
but make it entertaining"
she's read every paragraph
now the whole pub is vibrating
you can really make the whole scene vital
with the Mark E. Smith Curmudgeon Bible

A scowl toward the barman

and a sneer for every patron

they didn't really want to leave

but it's clear she's gonna make 'em

vitriol coated thin in jest

swiping drinks out of hands – no hint of reparation

and the prophet'll swear black is white

just to send you into a spiral

in the Mark E. Smith Curmudgeon Bible

Page 96, psalm 25:

"You must test everyone.

find out what their weakness is

and send 'em on the run

dress it up as a holy mission

but mostly it's just fun"

it's lain unused for five years

now there's a supernatural revival

of the Mark E. Smith Curmudgeon Bible

Life is Full of Surprises

Imagine my surprise
the day I discovered that
when people talk about the "rat race"
There is no racing
and there are no rats involved whatsoever

Imagine my surprise
when the penny dropped
that "Octopus Energy"
is nowhere near as exciting as it sounds

Imagine my surprise
to learn that my nan's night time cocoa
doesn't lurk inside the husk
of a big hairy nut
but does end up inside a lairy old nutter

Imagine my surprise
when I was reliably informed
that it *is* safe to go to the beach
as that's not what a "fish tank" is after all

Imagine my surprise

at the revelation

that when people talk about "eighties pop"

this is not a niche genre

consisting entirely of octogenarian singers

Imagine my surprise

and my disappointment too

when my mental image

of The Badminton Horse Trials

was shattered by an explanation

from a friend. Now ex

Imagine my surprise

when someone mentioned "water polo"

then shot

my excitable

submersible

equine

questions

down

before they were even asked

Pips

Are you a pip?

I'm a pip

and the apple is my cosmos

The average apple

has around eight pips

and that's enough

to be getting on with

Watch out!

Worm!

Self Storage

I passed a building on Turner Road
called Big Yellow Self Storage
"That's a bit o' me" I thought
and felt suitably encouraged

I'll pop in there on my way back past
and book up a little space
I won't need much; well a little more
since my belly came on apace

Storage of the self
such a great idea
like that tortoise off Blue Peter
I'll come back another year

Set an alarm for five years hence
nah, sod it, make it six
hopefully that's time enough
for the world to find a fix

See, it's just too much

the grind and jerk
of incessant bad news
of forced leisure
in the reprieves from work

Running on empty for the past few years
punishing myself with junk food and beer
a permanent existential crisis
everything's fucked
however you slice it

So, on Monday
I'm gonna check myself in
store myself, hibernate
press pause on the self
and liberate my brain
from this circular, drainward thinking
the coriolis effect
all goodness stuck in the U-bend
to perpetually ferment
hair, fat, hate, gloop
it's a depressive soup
with no benefit to me

it spilled all down my favourite T

now you can all see it

it's too rancid to ignore

self storage

self storage

while there's still some self to store

Your Medals

You're a messy eater
you're a pig at the trough
you see those ketchup stains?
well, they won't come off!

We can track your movements
and trace you door to door
by the trail of splats and crumbs
that you've left all across the floor

Your shirt is spotted
with orange, peach, and blueberry
you should wring the damn thing out
it's effectively a smoothie

Sometimes we run a book
on the nature of your dollops
the composition of your sweatshirt's
like a bloody Jackson Pollock

There are crisps in your collar

there's Thai on your tie
and you're an adult man
so I don't know why

You've got egg on your elbow
and elsewhere, no doubt
it's a source of fascination
how you keep missing your mouth

There's mustard, and there's custard
amongst the medals that you wear
there's jam and mayonnaise
You're looking far from debonair

Coffee, tea, wine, and stout
some strands of cheese you grated
you've fought in all the food campaigns
and you're culinarily decorated

Flies!

I received a message this morning
an email, a text; I forget which
to inform me that I'd been sent
a most unusual package

I've not slept much lately
and I'm feeling kinda fried
but I think it said Ben Green
had sent me a box of flies

Now, even in my addled state
I can see that's pretty weird
but I do know a Ben Green
in fact, I've known him for years

We went to school together
from the age of five or six
and even now, in different towns
we keep in touch a bit

But why would he send me such a thing?

it really makes no sense

flies!

of all things!

what's he on?!

it's got me quite perplexed

But in the background, I knew I'd find

some dusty clue in my dusty mind

I cast back to some childhood jest

so brief, but now I've retrogressed

and find myself, aged eleven

in my once favourite jeans

the denim faded by design

iron-on patches on the things

After a lot of rough and tumble

of boyhood games and larks

the two sides of my front zip

suddenly pulled themselves apart

And every time I tugged the slider

to pull the teeth together

within seconds my pants were peeking out

as those teeth once more untethered

Of course, my mates found this hilarious

and fell around in bits

roaring in hysterics

shouting "*Flies!*", and wouldn't quit

My mum put in a new zip

that very Tuesday evening

then the whole thing was forgotten

well, maybe not the feeling

of being the butt of the joke

if only for an afternoon

it tasted like something

I didn't want to try again too soon

So, this package from Ben Green

is it a reference to that day?
I can't believe a grown man
would want to make me feel that way
again

As we've aged, I've just assumed
that the lads had all forgotten
my embarrassment and frustration
that left me so woe begotten

But what if they'd all made a pact
before they rode home for their tea
to wait for nigh on thirty years
then bring it back to me

They must have known how deep it cut
and not have been true friends
just used me like some jester
to pay comedic dividends

It knocked the wind right out of my sails

and kicked my life askew

such cruel and callous treatment

from someone you thought you knew

I head into the kitchen

while no one is about

and make myself some coffee

that tastes like old tile grout

Then deflated and defeated

I slope back to my desk

though the caffeine's perked me up a bit

I'm awake but still depressed

I log back into the system

check my emails, as you do

and spot one headed

"Ben Green has dropped off files for you"

It's Inevitable

Like a shocking hangover
from a quick midweek drink
like the realisation
you're the weakest link
like a fridge full of rotten
but well-intentioned vegetables
it's inevitable

like a dog eyeing up
an unguarded pork chop
like a crusty punk shouting
"fuck the cops!"
like your favourite jeans
not being *that* stretchable
it's inevitable

Like a seagull
dive-bombing you for your chips
like Michael McIntyre
getting on your tits
like an MPs position

just not being tenable

it's inevitable

Like being stitched up

in the really small print

like January

being four weeks of skint

like this poem ending

in the word "inevitable"

it's inevitable

Stretch

Stretch your hamstrings
and stretch your arms
stretch your back
your wrists and calves

Touch your toes
if you think you can
hip flexors crunch
the crunch of the damned

Everything's tighter
than it should be
sitting at this desk'll
be the death of me

Stretch today
and stretch mañana
the only splits I can do
are bananas

The Diet is Going Really Well

The diet is going really well
I've turned the gluttonous tide
I'm gonna be like Jim Morrisons
and break on through to the Mother's Pride

Ice creamed at you
'til I was blueberry muffin in the face
I think you might need an ear crumpet
to tell you the vermouth, you're deaf as a roast
and you can like it, or sugar lump it

And stop trying to butter me up
fish fingering for information
omeletteing you have your say
and you won't curry favour with that libation!

'Cos the diet is going really well
I'm not telling porkie pies
I wouldn't Eton mess you about

with something that's pie-in-the-sky

You've been taking hotpot shots at the trifle range
I think I'd like a pizza that, mate
I'll meet you there on fried slice day
and please don't be chocolate

I took my hotdog for a walk round the park
in a duffel, like Puddington Bear
Cheeses Christ! It was as cold as choc ice
I'm not going back bacon out there!

Yeah, the diet is going really well, thanks
I resist all bad foods, and their gravies
there's no need to be sour dough
just 'cos my legs have turned to jelly, baby

You're just like a beer with a sore head
you say I dream about food every day
don't get yourself in a lager, mate
just whelk away

Premature Reports About the Death of Punk

If you want to know what's killing punk; it's your fear

and your tedious obsession with a holy year

and it's the pedestal you put the past on

a real punk wouldn't rest their arse on that

you boring twat

it's not even your habitat

you're an infrequent flyer, and that's a fact

an annual apparition gone

just

like

that

A belly full of lager and a bladder full of piss

it's your annual bout of rebelliousness

and it's pure nostalgia, a temporal cast-off

a teenage you would've laughed your arse off

you jokers are no better

than the teds that went before ya

who you used to sneer at

for dressing quasi-Edwardian

and their quiffs were thinner than racing snakes

and their drainpipes were blocked with pies and cake

Every summer, squeeze into your bondage kecks

jump in the motor and off you trek

to the seaside, an unloved B-side

but now there's somewhere to hide

in a crowd, where the music's loud

and you won't be cowed

Like you are in the rest of your miserable life

When you pull up in the car at your annual gig

do the doors fly off and the wheels look sick?

as they keel over at ninety degrees

and the exhaust over-eggs its pop and wheeze

when you've walked halfway to the venue

does a nagging thought upend you?

that you've left behind your plastic bucket of glitter

your red nose, bowtie, and squirty flower

does your big red mouth turn down to a frown?

'cos you, my friend, are a day-trippin' clown

Four days later the nostalgia bubble bursts
but you still need another two weeks off work
to grow back the sides of your hair
and ensure there's no dye left in there
flatten the rest and trim it back
'cos you can't go back to work like that
HR would have you in for a chat
Janice on reception would choke on her Kit Kat

Now I'm not perched on my private Mount Sinai
passing down the ten punk commandments
on The Lurkers, The Damned, Splodgenessabounds
on your age, or your hair, or your garments
but you want to seal it in amber
and break it out just once a year
we all can be prone to nostalgia
but let me make a few things clear
your youthful ideals, you threw out to rot
or maybe you just forgot:

It's always been about the underdog
not punching down, but punching up
it's not supposed to be a museum piece
whose relevance has all but ceased
that "kid" you berate for being "woke"
has more punk in his veins than some bitter old bloke
playing at fancy dress once a year
getting pissed up on plastic glass beer
you ain't liked a new band since 1982
just get off yer arse and huff some glue

You've become everything punk was against
you gradually slipped to the wrong side of the fence
using tabloid attack, not reasoned defence
no sense of compassion, or intelligence
you say you're still a rebel? Don't make me laugh
you do nothing for the scene, just talk out o' yer arse
you think you're an authority
but you're an amateur
it's just cosplay now, you're a caricature

#1 Fan

Round and round we go

our relationship speeds up

our relationship slows down

but spinning, almost always spinning

We create our own microclimate

of love and mutual respect

we heat up, we cool down

way down

I get the chills

hairs stand on end

porcupine arms

goosebumps

temperature animals

Your slender torso

enticing protrusions of action and adventure

you're a whirling dervish

our safe word tattooed above your left nib

I don't recall when you entered my life

it's like you've always been there

summertime yearning

electric, and yielding, without complaint

to my whims

After all that's transpired

and the receipt has expired

you're still my number one fan

FFFPRRRT

Fogg

An 'all you can eat' Chinese buffet

I went at it like a hog

around Ma Wong's in eighty trays

and now I'm Bilious Fogg

All Work is Factory Work

All work is factory work
I know this to be true
stuff comes in, stuff goes out
it don't matter what you do
subtract your sleeping hours
your work, and your commute
and you'll find there really aren't
that many hours left for you

And those hours that you cling to
do you use them as you'd like to?
or is your tank near-drained
exhausted body?
exhausted brain?
all your minutes, hours, days and weeks
subject to time and motion critiques
how productive can you be
when you've been squeezed
and squeezed
and squeezed
and squeezed?

It's savagery, and it's a waste
real lives switched for paste
stifled by drudge, living a grudge
your hopes and your dreams outpaced
nobody really wants to be here
nobody really wants to be here

Nine long years in the factory
I thought I'd "escaped", but the joke's on me
'cos the colour of your collar
and what you do for your dollar
makes no real difference in the end
it drives us all round the fucking bend
face it; we're all debased
just in slightly different ways
manual or cerebral, an insidious evil
that leaves us with a sour aftertaste

All jobs are dirty
none of them clean
and we're all fed through
the same sausage machine

all pinned by an omnipotent capitalist entomologist
like butterflies on a card
trying to preserve something he just netted
and killed

To continue on this path, I am no longer willing
'cos this is existing, not living

Bryan Adams

Why not be a DJ
get a gig in a local pub
go all around the town
and put some posters up
be nice and clear
about what you're gonna play
funk, soul, northern, Latin
and Motown all the way

The first hour's pretty desolate
the whole night's on the skids!
but soon the place is full
of music-hungry hominids
tapping feet and nodding heads
there ain't no dancing yet
'cos we're British and we need
to get a few beers down our necks

Two hours in and the place is heaving
with drinkers, and dancers as well
some Bobby Byrd, some Doris Troy

they're under the Technics' spell
a bloke in a tight Fred Perry
asks about the previous tune
I gladly tell him it's Don Gardener's
My Baby Likes to Boogaloo

It's a good job my mate is driving
as I'm being plied with drinks
he's on medication
so it's not as selfless as you might think
but libations keep arriving
and I feel like a demi-god
although I know that's pretty daft
'cos I'm just putting some records on

But there is a skill, there is an art
in choosing the right sounds to impart
in giving people something new
that they haven't heard, but will dance to
I *could* simply play the tried and tested
tunes in which we're all invested
fish in a barrel?
it'd be easy

But frankly, that's no fun for me

That said, I'm not too precious
and I'll play some well known tunes
to get 'em on the dancefloor
then slip in something obscure
I keep in mind it's a pub gig
with a well-mixed clientele
not everyone here's a record nerd
but there are some in; I can tell

OVO? Not needed here*
it's the tunes that carry weight
two grand for a forty-five?
I'll take a twelve quid repress, mate
I might be spinning funk and soul
but I'm a punk at heart
and the snobbery of the soul scene
makes gatekeeping an art

There's always one, and here she comes
staggering towards the decks
she'll probably ask for *The Snake*

or some other overplayed request
"Have you got any Bryan Adams?"
well, I confess I'm taken aback
what with this being a soul night
and that being something that Bryan lacks

I apologise, I don't know why
'cos there're posters all round the gaff
I patiently explain it's a soul night
(I don't add "and *Bryan Adams is crap!*")**
"It's soul, and funk, and Motown, and stuff
so that's what's in the box"
she's mega-drunken and perplexed
but eventually wanders off

James Brown and Gene Chandler
The Soul Searchers and Billy Garner
Chuck Womack & The Sweet Souls
Hank Mance, Jack Hammer, and Butterballs
Marlena Shaw and Sharon Jones
James Coit and Sugar Pie DeSanto
Larry Williams & Johnny Watson
Otis Lee, Ann Alford and Billy Thompson

The room's now brimming with joyous feeling

and sweat's dripping off of the artexed ceiling

the landlord's grinning, he's making a killing

and revelling in all the spinnin' and swillin'

it's the best day's takings he's ever seen

and he takes some photos of the fantastic scene

whacks 'em on his insta and tags his mate, Dean

to show the lazy article where he *could've* been

I see the crowd part at the back of the room

then like a zip undone it moves on through

the gap closes behind, and there stood at the alter

is the lady from earlier, propped up by her daughter

just half an hour from our first encounter

she's not spoken yet, but I know she's bound to

by the way that her kid looks so embarrassed

she says *"Have you got any Bryan Adams?"*

*For the uninitiated, OVO = original vinyl only. Some soul events will only allow their DJs to play the very first – i.e. the original - pressing of a record. Prices for many of these originals are hundreds, and even thousands of pounds, so that's way out of my league (plus I'd be frightened to play them!)

**very restrained

One of Our Idiots is Missing

One of our idiots is missing
I think we lost him by the fountain in the square
if you spot him, apprehend him
if he's too big, fold and bend him
but please do not return him to our care

One of our idiots is missing
you may find him talking loudly in the pub
holding forth on immigration
and the state of this great nation
or maybe he'll be passed out in some shrubs

One of our idiots is missing
We lost him in the lizard/chemtrails mist
shouting "wake up, you damn sheeple!"
and you really must be heedful
'cos he hasn't got a clue what research is

One of our idiots is missing
you can try to seize him if you think you must
you may find him on the main drag

draped in a bloody big flag

'cos the Daily Mail has turned his brain to mush

One of our idiots is missing

he can't be hard to capture if you try

you can find him any weekday

saying things he says you can't say

'cos cognitively he's in short supply

One of our idiots is missing

and we just want to say a big "amen!"

he thinks he's quite delightful

but he's ignorant and spiteful

and we never want to see the twat again

Muy Feliz Pescado!

He seemed a little depressed
so, I let the goldfish out
his name is Brian, I ain't lyin'
he's riddled with existential doubt

I let him out of the goldfish flap
to stretch his fins, an' tail, an' that
obviously, I had to flood the house
to ease his Piscean passage out

It was a usual British summer
and had been pissing down for days
the six inches of water
brought a smile to his fishy face

Darting round the barbeque
then around that old creosote tin
he swam a circuit round the washing line
then another around the bins

By the toes of the Buddha statue

he pulled up with a swish
as if searching for some spiritual guidance
but who knows with a fish?

The Spanish lady from next door
popped her head over the fence
spotted Brian, pointed, and smiled
with pleasure, so intense

"Muy feliz pescado!"
her eyes were shining bright
"Muy feliz pescado!"
and do you know what?
she was right

Bacon Ninja

Vince is a vacillating veggie
his vulnerable vows inflict a constant wedgie
on the views he espouses
Turkey Twizzlers in his trousers
clandestine creeping?
gorging on game in your garden
he's a useless bacon ninja
with a hardon for lardons

Stealthily scoffs scotch eggs by the score
promises himself he won't eat no more
chewin' on chicken in Chalfont St Giles
to avoid getting caught he'll travel for miles
bolting beef bhuna in a Bradford backstreet
his shame is outweighed by his mania for meat
pigging Pepperamis in Peterborough city
he's got a bag o' the things, and boy it ain't pretty

Bingeing on beefburgers behind the bins
thinks he's being stealthy, but we've all clocked him
snaffling a sausage in a pseudo-savage style

in an alleyway in Aldwych, or a carpark in Argyle
chompin' on a chump chop like a chang'd up chimp
hiding in the shadows with the girls and their pimps
pouncing on a pork pie like a pissed-up pelican
hiding in a bush at the Gardens of Heligan

Nobody's perfect, ain't that the truth, son
but don't badge yourself for the sake of illusion
'cos you ain't fooling no one; it just won't do
munching meaty morsels like a half-starved raccoon

The Idiot Convention

A flock of loudly honking geese
in suite to suite migration
graze the buffet with consummate ease
still in their V- formation

Beaks clacking incessantly
like ancient football rattles
I slip off to the hotel bar
to evade the corporate prattle

Nigel, the new goose from Accounts
is about to deliver his seminar
on fiscal issues he'll surmount
fancies himself as a commissar

Or, alternatively, in suite three
we've Wendy in from marketing
hoping that her PowerPoint
is really gonna rock the joint

Look at that joker

straight as a poker

it's Oliver, from HR

a boring turd

a spirit choker

I'd have had him barred

With his stale jokes and wacky socks

he thinks himself a character

but with a lurid shirt and tie combo

he's just a joy prohibitor

Bright colours often serve

as a smokescreen for the malady

a convenient alternative

to a genuine personality

in the corporate world

it's good advice

you should take it

no rules, just improvise

In the breaks, beaks clattering

about the current primetime

Saturday TV monstrosity

as if it has anything to offer

beyond a convenient timeslot

ideal for those with young kids

but in all honesty, subjecting kids to this drivel

should warrant a visit from social services

and the sooner the better

It's abuse

its goose abuse

well, *gosling* abuse

I prefer "gooselets" myself

it might not be a real word

but let's not be slaves to convention

With Anti Cimex legend (and PI$$ER / Körd Värld bandmate), Charlie Claesson, in Älvängen, Sweden circa 2016. A trip to record some vocals on the Bring the Drones *Ignorance Paradise* album. Photo by Fatima.

The Domestics with III Guerra outside The Library Pub, Oxford on the final date of our joint four day weekender. A great band, and really nice guys from Mallorca, Spain. Martí sadly died in a motorcycle crash in 2019.
On steps top to bottom: Rhodes, Me, Luis, Mint, Bernat. Front row L-R: Martí (RIP), Mark, Simon. Photo by Pete Marler.

At Bambos Fest 2015. At the much-loved, and now sadly defunct, T Chances venue in Tottenham, London. Always a lot of messy fun at those T Chances gigs...total carnage most of the time! Photo by John Marshall.

Totally bug-eyed at Entombed Fest, Hastings, 2023. Photo by Mark Richards.

March

Frog trumpeter marches extravagantly
legs lift high
flapping flippers slap onto the pavement
two gorillas, a bass drum apiece
deliver a violent, primal beat
six lemurs gad, bound, and caper
spilling trilled notes from piccolos
a trio of cats on skateboards
swipe-tinkle triangles seemingly at random
purely for their own amusement

A grizzly bear in half-moon spectacles
honks lustily on a tuba
whilst a bloodhound in a bobble hat
puffs heartily, but silently, at a whistle
a quartet of rhinos beat
a migraine-inducing tattoo on their shiny snares
and the golden lion
resplendent in red hat and cape
leads the procession proudly
through the deserted streets

Roadkill

It's fair to say you were here first
and I feel pretty bad about it
tarmac snaking through your manor
where I see you burst and split

Blood-matted fur and feathers
inside on the out
in clement, or inclement, weather
on verges hereabout

But all the sorrow that I feel
for your untimely end
won't pry me from the steering wheel
so with my conscience I contend

We've come too far to reverse now
we're hooked on steel and throttle
and irrespective of my qualms
the genie's truly out 'o the bottle

There's only one solution

'cos we're stolid like the rocks

a road safety course for the animals!

teaching applicants must speak fox

or badger

or pigeon

or pheasant

or deer

or squirrel

or rabbit

And if this ever happens

let me make one thing clear:

this was my bloody idea

© James Domestic, y'hear?

Let's Have Another Lockdown

Let's have another lockdown
I'll do it right next time
I'll go out jogging every day
not gorge on beer and wine

Let's have another lockdown
and I'll make the best of it
I'll cut the biscuits, crisps, and cheese
and perhaps my jeans will fit

Let's have another lockdown
I'll take an online class
improve myself with knowledge
not sit and grow my arse

Let's have another lockdown
no, not the horrible stuff
just the slowing and reflecting
old priorities rebuffed

Let's have another lockdown

I really wouldn't mind

go out and get a six pack

but this time the other kind

Do For You

If you're confused and feeling lost
then I'll supply a map
if you cannot bear the cost
then I'll give you what I have

If you're drifting on the seas
I'll gladly lend my anchor
I'll grab the wheel, and turn the keel
to avoid that supertanker

If you're caught in an earthquake
I will pull you from the rubble
and if what I offer's not enough
then my efforts will be doubled

If you're floating in the ether
and you want to come down
like a cowboy I'll lasso you
and pull you closer to the ground

If you're stuck, deep in a rut

of indecision and doubt

let me grab my JCB

so I can scoop you out

If you feel too healthy

I'll feed you full of chips

if you feel misanthropic

I'll arrange the apocalypse

If you feel too analogue

I'll gladly digitise you

if your life's become predictable

then I'll try to surprise you...

...

...

...

...

...

...

...

...

...

BOO!

Celebrate Your Youth

Celebrate your youth
you thought that bloke was long in the tooth
when he was 31
but I tell ya mate, the worst's yet to come
so, celebrate your youth
you don't know it but you're almost bulletproof
I speak the truth, so celebrate your youth

You'll pine for it once it's gone
and it didn't even last that long
you'll get to 48 and have a string of car-crash dates
with needy goth barmaids a fraction of your age
you'll buy a Harley Davidson
you can't even get the leathers on
false freedom and elation
smeared across the central reservation
don't jump off the roof, dad!

And every time you hear that song
you'll wonder where it all went wrong
and you're struggling to understand

this fast-expanding waistband

every ache and pain

you try to numb it with cocaine

but now you need it every fucking day

and you're like a catholic at communion

joining the queue at the back

wearing a false moustache

to claim another wafer

you didn't even like the first one!

and your kids all fucking hate ya!

yeah, your kids all fucking hate ya!

hahaha!

Your kids all fucking hate ya!

When you're young you've got some licence

to act up, and that's fine

as it's the folly of youth

that brand new tooth

well it might just get you off the hook

and that's the truth

don't take my word for it

you go too far and you're gonna do bird for it

but just be smart and forge a path of your own

and just enjoy it while you've got it

'cos one day you'll have lost it

if your parents don't get it

tell 'em to buy a caravan and fuck off!

Fuck off!

here we go again...

Celebrate your youth

you thought that bloke was long in the tooth

when he was 31

but I tell ya mate, the worst's yet to come

So, celebrate your youth

you don't know it but you're almost bulletproof

I speak the truth, mate

so celebrate your youth, mate

Your eyes will never see that way again

so savour it and taste it

or else you're gonna waste it, like we all do

experience is useful

but it tends to make you bitter and cynical

and your sense of wonder minimal at best

You think I jest?

I'm just getting some shit off my chest

'cos age in many ways is just a curse

and we all blunder

wanting to be younger when we're older

and older when we're younger

so, youth don't blunder

don't knuckle under the weight of expectation

don't listen to me, or anyone of my generation

celebrate it

celebrate it

celebrate your glorious youth

Celebrate Your Youth is a song that originally appeared on a 12"
called *The Five Curses* by Domestic Curse in 2022. Domestic Curse is
an electronic project I do with Curse (aka John Hewson, ex-The 5
String Dropout Band, and currently in The Jabberwocky Prayers). The
"*Don't jump off the roof, dad!*" line was a nod – I initially thought –
to the late actor and narrator, Bernard Cribbins. I subsequently
realised that I was actually thinking of Tommy Cooper and his 1961
single that I must have heard growing up on some oldies station my
parents listened to, as it was already a very old record by the time I
was born. Stuck in the ol' noggin somehow though. A comedy song
about suicide was bound to, I guess!

Courier Bastards

Its contents are really important
so I've stayed indoors all day
I've received an assortment of messages
to assure me it's on its way
now I dare not leave the hallway
in case I should miss the drop
so I've dehydrated myself entirely
and I haven't fed the dog

A series of pings throughout the day
updating me on its E.T.A.
each one much later than the last
and I paid for 'Express', so I could get it fast!

Nine, ten, eleven o'clock, twelve
no knock!
one, two, three o'clock, four
no knock!
I'll have my nose to the bloody window all night

If I've been a little vague

then let me be explicit

I'll go on a bloody rampage

if I turn my back and miss it

the non-delivery of this consignment

will lead to my mental misalignment

where I'll take on a new assignment

to dish out courier-based violence

It's 8pm, and I'm bloody livid

a knock at the door – could this finally be it?

my fists are clenched, and my face is tight

I'll open the door and I'll punch out their lights!

but no; it's my neighbour from 74

"Did you know you have a parcel

sat by your back door?"

Turns out it's been there since 11 this morn

in the wind and the rain, and it's now quite forlorn

I thought I was a sentinel that nothing could pass

but those courier bastards have got me outclassed

Death to the Peach!

Apparently my diet is woeful
and lacks fibre and vitamins
so I promised my GP I'd eat more fruit
and this week I'm gonna begin

I shall grapple with an apple
arrange for an orange
I'll try to charm a banana
and then we will see who's in charge

I've not had much time for berries
but I guess I can give 'em a go
logan, rasp, blue, and straw
and any others that I come to know

I've recently become aware
of the joy in a juicy, ripe pear
in the office, the juice of a plum
has ruined my white shirt, and then some
I've tried taking mango and guava
but peeling 'em's quite a palaver

and on a works outing to the Isle of Thanet

I was sorely disappointed by a pomegranate

Now my lunchbox is stocked with easy peelers

I have apples and grapes, at every meal

and here's some advice

if you want it or not

if you're eating at home

or in a restaurant

whether solo, or as part of some liaison

if you reach for a peach

please wear an apron

'Cos those juicy bastards

will assail you

and your sense of composure

and style will fail you

Death to the peach!

I Used to be Fucking Cherubic

Suspend your disbelief

press pause on your laughs

while I regale you with tales

of my adorable past

whilst my bearing may be

of one beaten with sticks

let's be clear

I used to be fucking cherubic

I'm blotched with colours

I didn't think human

I'm half-finished, discarded

and lacking in lumen

both angular and lumpy

like a product of Ernő Rubik

but I'll tell you, girl

I used to be fucking cherubic

Now my countenance is perturbing

if not downright disturbing

I'm like a discarded prop

hanging round the lot

of an unreleased film

by Stanley Kubrick

but I'm telling you all

I used to be fucking cherubic

My grades have slipped

the reviews have tanked

my skin is marbled

and my hair is lank

I make no sense

by any rubric

but please believe me

once, I was fucking cherubic

The Gig of Their Lives

They played the gig of their lives
those kids
they played the gig of their lives
been here for the soundcheck
since half-past five
but they played the gig of their lives

The crowd fell in love
with every song they'd written
the promoter, with their paltry fee
has now gone missing
the singer's selling merch to folk
as fast as he can
the sweat stings his eyes
but don't crash his élan

They played the gig of their lives
those kids
they played the gig of their lives
to a half-full pub on a Thursday night
they played the gig of their lives

Now they need to find the people
that are letting them crash
they can't afford a hotel
and the van heater's crap
there're only eighty people
but it's not the size
of the audience
but the size of the good time, right?

They played the gig of their lives
those kids
they played the gig of their lives
tomorrow there's another 300 mile drive
but they played the gig of their lives tonight
yeah, they played the gig of their lives

Sweat poured from the ceiling
in rivulets
and despite not knowing
how the lyrics went
the noise they made
was both raw, and saintly
and the congregated eighty

were blessed and sated

They played the gig of their lives
those kids
they played the gig of their lives
they'll play anywhere and nowhere
just any ol' dive
and they'll play the gig of their lives
you'll probably never hear 'em
they'll split up and die
but they played the gig of their lives
those kids
and they do it every single time

Office Revolution Day

I can't be arsed
with this crap today
it'll probably
be ditto tomorrow
and I strongly suspect
all of next week
and the months
and the years to follow

I can't be arsed
with this crap today
I've reached the end
of my tether
apparently this is
what life's about
the past
the present
forever

I can't be arsed
with this crap today

I've finally had enough
so stick your spreadsheet
up your arse
and find some other mug

The monitor's
goin' out of the window
the mouse is now
housed in the shredder
taped a prawn
under the MDs drawers
that'll be a top stink-spreader

Never again
will I need to buy pens
I've ransacked the stationery cupboard
my bag is bulging
with contraband
I don't even care
if I'm discovered

Ran a key down the flank
of the CEOs car

and it's no more than he deserves

treat your staff badly

and one day you'll find

that one of those worms

has turned

And if one worm turns

will another follow?

will the photocopier

be in bits tomorrow?

will the phone lines be cut

and hostages taken?

will this capitalist enterprise

be forever forsaken?

will middle-managers

be stapled to their desks

by their ears?

or sellotaped to the ceiling fans

whirling round in fear?

What will it take?

I ask *what will it take?*

Crocs Are a Gateway Drug

Don't wear crocs
they're a gateway drug
they do more harm than smack
you sordid mugs

Polymer monstrosities
designed by a crayon-wielding child
snot bubbling out of its nose
dripping in unspeakable goo
croc child, snot child
euuurrrghh, I'd rather not, child

And once you succumb
to the crocodile's smile
you're slippin' and inch
then you're slippin' a mile
your style?
vile!

Next it'll be beige slacks
with an elastic waistband

a practical red fleece

it soon gets out of hand

Before you know where you are

you're ordering stuff

out of those little catalogues

in the back of the Sunday papers

a commemorative World War 2 shoehorn

a hideous plate

with "The People's Princess" on it

a scale model of Ronnie Corbett

food prep gadgets you use once

and consign to the drawer of doom

and truth be told

you haven't got the room

So, don't buy crocs

they're hard to recycle

they make you look like a cartoon

and not a cool one either

it's a downhill trajectory

the slipperiest slope

you've lost your balance

on the style tightrope

Now, my wardrobe is hardly á la mode
but there's a line over which I just won't go
and those horrors shout sartorial strife, and
"Chuck me in the waiting room for the afterlife"
you know I'll declare it until my last breath
crocs are a gateway to an early death
worse than smack
worse than crack
'cos they're pernicious like cigarettes
and everywhere, like trans fats
and they're here now, so it kind of seems OK
but it's not OK
OK?

Three thousand, seven hundred psi
that's a lot of force for the weak to fight
but fight it you must
'cos its right, and it's just
treat with contempt, and eye with mistrust
'cos crocs are a gateway drug
oh yeah, crocs area gateway drug

Just before I really dived headlong into punk and hardcore. Aged around 14. Bit of a hair metal phase. Leaning on my late father's gold Granada. The Ford Pinto in the background we brought from a guy who not long after was 'stung' on *The Cook Report* (ask yer dad!). When the show was aired we all watched it in the pub (not that I was going in pubs at 14, obviously, officer!). Photographer unknown.

What a poser! Another from that hair metal phase. Me 'n' dad got a bonnet scoop from an old Pontiac Transam, cut a hole in the Pinto's bonnet and grafted it on, like you do. Photographer unknown.

Even now, I don't need asking twice to pose for a photo! Haha! Spain 2022. Photo by Lucy James.

Aged 20. Playing with Me109's. This was taken in our local boozer in Great Clacton, a two minute walk from the flat I shared with bass player, Dave Morris. Three quarters of us were on the dole at time, and all liked a drink, so were totally happy to play for a decent-sized bar tab. Photographer unknown.

FOR INFORMATION PHONE:
(0255) 432.895 or
(0255) 431408

BAMBI ON ICE.

My very first band, when I was at school, was called Tantrum! (after the song by German thrashers, Tankard), we then changed our name to The Sly, and then The Jesus Suite. It was the same band, and songs, for each name (Me on guitar, Andy Hicks on bass, Nikki Alves on drums, and Andy 'Wardy' Ward on vocals. I remember drawing this cassette cover for our second demo whilst at school, when I probably should have been in a lesson. They were lucky I was even on the premises; I very often wasn't!

91

I'd thought all of these photos were lost forever, but Nikki found a few. This is us in our *Tantrum!* days. L-R: Andy Hicks, Me, Andy 'Wardy' Ward, and Nikki Alves. We're all still in touch even though we're spread around a bit (London, Suffolk, Wiltshire, and Australia). I still see Andy and Wardy a couple of times a year (Nikki not so much as she's the one in Oz). We'd have been approximately sixteen here. Photo by Stewart Turner.

Obligatory *band against a graffitied wall* shot. Photo by Stewart Turner.

Under Clacton Pier for mood. My shift away from rock and metal towards hardcore punk evidenced via my Electro Hippies hoody. I still look like Slash on a bad day though. L-R: Me, Wardy, Andy, Nikki. Photo by Stewart Turner.

Still lurking under the pier. Flasher macs in full effect! We never really did that much as a band, and we were pretty clueless really – a few local gigs, but I wouldn't change trade those times for anything. Photo by Stewart Turner.

Here Comes the Mirror, Man

If you look in the mirror
and there's nothing to please ya
if you stare long and hard
and think *"who is this geezer?"*
there's a stranger looking back
that you don't recognise
he's got peanuts for teeth
and bags for his eyes

His eyebrows are wiry
and out of control
it's hard to believe
all the hearts that he stole!
don't take it too hard
you can take it from me
you're probably not as stupid
and fat as you think

Your brain has a filter
and it makes things seems worse
you want to slam your whole life

into reverse

when I say "you"

and when I say "you're"

I mean it in general

not specific terms

they're not universal truths

to be run up the flagpole

and they don't apply to you

'cos you've always been awful

Look at His Mandibles

Look at his mandibles
waggling about
that's a happy critter
of that I have no doubt
he appeared beside me
on a bench in the park
then started nibbling heartily
at my ancient bookmark

I was on my lunch break
relaxing in the sun
away from the screen
and electric hum
a paperback
taking me far away
stepping out of the picture
in the midst of the day

Taking a nibble
and then staring up
the bookmark was tatty

so I didn't care that much
then *"Oi! Mate!*
Can't you take a hint?!"
Give us a bit
of your cheese sandwich!"

I was properly stunned
as anyone would be
if a beetle started yakking
by your side on a seat
he said *"Perk up, chum*
now you know the secret
that beetles can talk
and I'd be obliged if you keep it"

"Yeah, sure" I replied
not believing my eyes
or my ears for that matter
well, you can imagine my surprise!

"Now, about that sandwich..."
he said, expectantly
I pinched off a crumb

and he wiggled with glee
his mouth-parts a-whirl
with cheddar and pickle
then he gave a great burp
and let out a loud whistle

The noise from my new friend
startled some pigeons
a scruffy-feathered gang
hanging out by a poo bin
in ragtag formation
they took to the sky
and one dropped a present
in the poor beetle's eye

Well, I say *"in his eye"*
but consider the scale
of a bird turd vs beetle
he got totally nailed
maybe he's just got some
crap in his mouth
I thought, as he slurred
and was hopping about

Shaking his tarsi
and shouting the odds
cursing each one
of the old beetle gods
then do you know
what he says to me?
"Did you know that us beetles
get legless on cheese?"

I confess, I did not
but it explained quite a lot
the sudden character change
the way he behaved

A lady beetle passes
and I politely tip my hat
he says *"Cor!*
Look at the carapace on that!!"
before I head back to the office
I give disappointed glances
a sexist beetle
now, what are the chances!

Onion

I'm writing a poem
about your onion-like qualities
but I'm concerned about the history
of onion-based poetry
and your expectation of what's to come
due to common tropes around the allium
used as a metaphor to suggest
that you're multi-layered and complex
and that gradually your layers may fall away
to reveal your core, your heart, someday

That you're a mystery
a conundrum
and far from being humdrum
that there's more to you
than could ever meet the eye
but these are exhausted analogies
and pray, do not pre-empt me, please
or I'll be taking odds
on who'll be first to cry

Maybe I should see a shrink

about the way I tend to think

'cos to you, an onion I make a link

because you make the whole gaff stink

Camping

I blame the drink
plus, I'm easily led
now I'm lying in a field
instead of my bed
Thursday night in the pub
half round the bend
with booze
I agreed to a camping weekend

I really hated camping
when I was a kid
now, as an adult
it's no wonder I did
it's just discomfort
for discomfort's sake
you call it an adventure
I call it insane

prostrate on the lumpy ground
buzzing mozzies by the lake
I knew before they picked me up

I'd made a big mistake
there's no actual adventure
it's just boring and damp
my arse has gone numb
and my leg has got cramp

"Living under canvas"
it's romanticised
by tedious wankers
that are dead inside
like those monks
that flagellate themselves
to know Christ's pain
camping's a similar hellish game

It must be a penance
for some previous sin
I'm never ever
gonna go camping again

It's like buying a fancy sandwich
then hiding pins in it
indoors was too good

you wanted something shit

some self-devised hardship

to make you feel alive

have you ever seen a shrink?

why not give it a try

It must be a penance

for some previous sin

I'm never ever

gonna go camping again

Cosh

It hits you like a brick
when you least expect it
knocks you for six
makes you feel like a right prick
like you popped your own balloon
bought another
and popped that one too

It's a bolt of lightning
it cleaves you in two
now you can't remember
which one's the "real" you
it's like stubbing your toe
and it hurts like hell
so you make sure
you stub the other nine as well

From the darkness, a cosh
smacks you square in the chops
sends you careening
and leaves you at a loss

desperate for answers
you dive into the gloom
to find the cosh wielder
is you

Others too

But mostly you

It hits you like a brick
when you least expect it
knocks you for six
makes you feel like a right prick
like you popped your own balloon
bought another
and popped that one too

The cosh wielder is you
yes, it's you

The Uninvited Guest

An uninvited guest
now you'll be put to the test
now your joy de vive
is under arrest

How long is enough
before you start to get tough
and commence deploying hints
that this visit should be snuffed?

You don't want to seem rude
they're a friend after all
but you had this time earmarked
and they didn't even call

Not that you'd have answered
you're a borderline recluse
but you could've texted back later
with some ingenious excuse

Is now the time to flick the domino

that knocks all the others to the floor?
to kick-off the hint events
that sees them out of the door?

Yeah
I think it's time
an hour ago you were poised
to open up a nice red wine
now it's hidden behind a cushion
and all you can think about
is what you're missing

That pizza you kicked under the sofa
will still be ok, but cold 'cos of this interloper
and on the table
that book you were going to start
and on the deck
Lee 'Scratch' Perry straight from the Black Ark

Yawn
cough
yawn some more
an exaggerated stretch

push the bolt on the back door
"*I must put the bin out in a minute*
before I hit the hay"
please take all these bloody hints
get up and on your way

"*So sorry I keep yawning,*
but I've had a full-on week"
please please please
just get off your arse and leave

The penny better drop now
or I'll get belligerent
don't just show up when you fancy
it feels like an affront

Please leave me in my bubble
of music, book, and wine
and I want to scoff that pizza
make a proper plan next time!

For God's Sake, Put Your Bloody Feet Away

The ugliest things I ever saw
like a bag of old spuds tipped on the floor
out of which your legs protrude
not one iota of pulchritude
the flakes, the cracks, the fungal blight
the very thought keeps me awake at night
the yellowing toenails, the bunions, the corns
the grisly countenance, like two lumps of brawn
your trotters are rotters, your plates are a state
For God's sake, put your bloody feet away

But all feet are hideous
none of 'em are nice
and you've no aesthetic acumen
if you think otherwise
don't want to see your crusty heels
as you turn and walk away
for God's sake, put your bloody feet away

Put 'em in foot prisons
to pay for their crimes

their felonies are an offence

to my poor weeping eyes

encase them in an upper

keep those hairy toes at bay

for God's sake, put your bloody feet away

Burn those Jesus creepers

and please do not delay

they're only category D*

the feet'll just escape

I've never been religious

but I'll get on my knees and pray

for God's sake, put your bloody feet away

Stick 'em in a trainer

Chelsea boot, or Cuban heel

a classic knee-length boot

or Dr Marten if you will

I saw you in your flip-flops

a crusty cheese buffet

for God's sake put your bloody feet away

*Category D is an open prison

With The Domestics in Volos, Greece, October 2019. L-R: Me, Mint, Rhodes, Simon. Photo by yours truly.

With The Domestics, having a pre-Poison Fest beer. Brighton, June 2022. L-R: Me, Simon, Rhodes, Mint. Photo by moi.

Crowdsurfed in Ipswich, 2018. For the life of me I can't recall how Simon, The Domestics' drummer, can be in the crowd (that's him bottom left) as I'm usually only crowdsurfed whilst we're playing! Photo by Miff Pleasant.

Surfin' again! This time at Manchester Punk Festival, 2017. Photo by Charlee Ramsey.

In the air again! This time at a Housing Coop in Ipswich, 2018. I think this is the gig we had filmed by our mate, Andy, to use for the 'Cherry Blossom Life' video. Photo by Dan Rutter.

Another from Manchester Punk Festival, 2017. Photo by Charlee Ramsey.

From a very early rehearsal with The Domestics at the Unit One rehearsal studio in Colchester. Around 2012/2013. Photographer unknown.

Playing the aftershow at the TNS Records 10th Anniversary gig in 2014. Luscious Locks! Haha! Photo by Tim 'Bev' Bevington

Why I Love Dub Pt. I

The bass moves right through you

that's how I'd describe it

like a warm, calming vibration

in the solar plexus

and I like it

oh, I like it

Plump round notes

in propulsive lazy waves

on which your body ebbs and flows

the tide is a loping, soothing tincture

a poultice of cyclical, healing nutrients

bathe in it

melt into its environment

a living thing

feel the pulse

and breathe

and breathe

and breathe

Every note counts

and you will feel them all

meditative

on another plane

in a different place

at a different pace

Space is food for thought

and the space in the bass

is where I eat

soul food

nourished

fulfilled

It's where I float

and drift

bass frequencies are a gift

a physical thing

it's where I think

and now I just am

this is as close to faith as I get

Defeat

What's the point in reading?
what's the point in thinking?
what's the point in holidays?
what's the point in sausages?
what's the point in boredom?
what's the point in fun?
what's the point in hoovering up
all those jammy dodger crumbs?

What's the point in smile?
what's the point in frown?
what's the point in in getting up?
what's the point in getting down?
what's the point in Jupiter?
what's the point in mars?
what's the point in wanky personalised
number plates on cars?

What's the point in alcohol?
what's the point in drugs?
what's the point in football?
what's the point in slugs?
what's the point in me?
what's the point in you?
what's the point in any fucking thing
we say and do?

What's the point in washing up?
what's the point in online banking?
what's the point in Christmas trees?

what's the point in wanking?
what's the point in beermats?
what's the point in soup?
what's the point in those
bloody 'orrible kiwi fruits?

What's the point in joining clubs?
what's the point in television?
what's the point in socialising?
what's the point in nihilism?
what's the point in this?
what's the point in that?
what's the point in hanging out with you
you boring twat?

What's the point in working?
what's the point in not?
what's the point in casual lurking?
what's the point in snot?
what's the point in flies?
what's the point in wasps?
what's the point in saying it is
when it patently is not?

What's the point in celebrity?
what's the point in politics?
what's the point in credibility?
what's the point in Weetabix?
what's the point in the judicial system?
what's the point in anything?
what's the point in being a bird
if you won't use your wings?

What's the point in time?

what's the point in space?
what's the point in this whole
bloody piss poor human race?

What's the point in Jesus?
what's the point in waste?
what's the point in even trying
to make a cogent case?

what's the point in_____
what's the point in_____
what's the point in_____
what's the point in_____
what's the point in_____
what's the point in_____
what's the point in_____
what's the point in_____

Ah, fill in the blanks yourself.

Air Con Con

It's a con
that air
racing out of that grille
in the name of comfort, but still
it's like fighting a biting icy wind
I can get that at home 'cos I live in England

I certainly don't need it
in this Philadelphia hotel
I want to reside in comfort
not some chilly, goosebump hell

And have you ever seen
a frozen concrete slab
have boiling water poured upon
and marvelled as it cracked?
that's me
when I walk in or out of this place
the temperature differential
feels like it's going to split my face

the lobby's like an icebox

but outside: a raging sun

it's like going from the tropics

to the north pole; it ain't fun

So yeah

it's a con that air

don't let anyone tell you otherwise

it's a tempest

it's the coldest

and the noise keeps you awake

all through the bloody night

*Honestly, I absolutely *hate* air con. Aside from the obvious environmental aspects, it's just horrible innit? It doesn't just mean a lower temperature on a hot day; it's like you've stepped through some kind of mad time vortex thing and are suddenly accompanying Shackleton on an ill-fated polar expedition. Makes me want to piss constantly too. Absolute dogshit if you ask me.

Not Me

You wanted to go

you longed to leave

your final furlong was a sentence

not a reprieve

and when your essence

seeps out across the floor

absorbed into the rug

or flowing beneath the door

then who would want to be here anymore?

not me

But there's no denying

you've left a space; a blank

but the shape of the missing

is a ten-years-past you

that's the you we remember

the you we shall recall

in our hearts

not the pills, the decline

and the hospital charts

not me

The chafing pulls

of resignation and frustration

that the you that you'd built

was now some poor relation

death was a reward

and when you tally the score

who would want to

live like that anymore?

not me

That Vet Who Was the Drummer in That Band

Don't make advances on that horse

it don't desire you for intercourse

leave it alone; be on your way

remember: neigh means neigh

Posters by Dave Morris and Pete Northam,
AKA 'Zippy' and 'Petals Menterstate'

In-between Tantrum! and Me.109's, I was in Krapp. Pete Northam, and Dave Morris (guitar and bass respectively) were a few years older than me and opened up the whole DIY thing for me – I have a lot to blame those two for! We're still mates, and I see 'em whenever The Domestics play Southampton, where they both now live. I joined Krapp when I was in the 6th form at school (I only stayed on for the extra two years so me and dad could keep the house for two more years after he and my mum got divorced), and we split a couple of years later.

Krapp's first studio demo: One Year of Krapp. Not sure why I ended up doing the cassette inlay, but that's all my own drunken work. Yep, all my fault. Must have taken all of three minutes! Haha!!!!

Me and Dave Morris in Krapp days. We didn't play many gigs as Krapp really, in the couple of years before it fizzled out. We did one in Bishops Stortford, where I was so drunk before we even got in the van that I forgot to switch my guitar amp on until midway through the second song! And I'm told we did one in Colchester, but I have no recollection of that at all! We did do one at Highfields holiday camp in aid of Albania, as I recall, that got recorded by the BBC, but sadly it didn't make us stars on the evening news. Mostly they were at The Holland Club (later The Tavern) in Holland-on-Sea (as above), or at The Lord Nelson in Clacton. I was probably eighteen in this pic. Photographer unknown.

Me and Pete Northam playing a Christmas gig with Krapp at The Lord Nelson in Clacton-on-Sea. Everyone dressed up, and the others bet me I wouldn't wear a dress for the gig...and let's face it, I look pretty sexy! Photographer unknown.

Back at The Holland Club. Dave in the same S.O.B. shirt as before. Me with a really shit guitar with Sid Vicious on it! Photographer unknown.

Unwanted Gift: Cement Boots

Cut your nose off to spite your face
the slowest runner in the human race
no real thought about the lane you choose
it must be hard to run
in those massive clown shoes

Fairy tale fictions really blew your mind
put a tick in a box for the very first time
didn't want to understand the consequences
'cos you felt like a soldier
fighting down in the trenches

No, you don't "know how things work"
and you really haven't done your "research"
sold on a soundbite nailed to a lie
painted a picture you felt you had to defy
but you didn't get your "freedom"
you just got less
and you dragged the whole lot of us
into this mess

you didn't know your onions

you had a xenophobic quess

with all the intelligence

of a punnet of cress

A narrow-margin "win" was the best you could do

And you're treating it like it's World War II

But actually you're pissing on

the legacy of that conflict

Churchill wanted Europe

to be a safer place to live in

not that I'm any great admirer of the geezer

starving Indians in their millions

a racist Ebeneezer

But that's not the focus here

I don't want to get off point

it's you Little England arseholes

and the fascists you appoint

that tell you they're just like you

sipping pints in the pub

but only for the cameras

then they're off to their private club

it's a photo op
it's a shallow ruse
but you shut your brain off
if it's pointed out to you

Haven't even got the decency
to admit you were wrong
can you really not hear
the bum notes in the song?
a rancid melody
a nonsensical harmony
soundtracking our descent
through the murky waters
in boots of cement

Don't Groom a Baboon

I heard you say
in a pub's back room
that your ambition
is to groom a baboon
but I'm not convinced
that you've thought it through
for once, I'm the voice of reason:
"*Please don't groom a baboon*"

And when you say "*grooming*"
I'm, of course, assuming
that you don't mean
in a Saville-esque way
but removing dust and ticks
and other assorted bits
sprucing up the monkey
for his monkeying day

Don't be fooled
by a comedic posterior
you really don't want

a baboon that near to ya

you'll end up filling your pantaloons

if you get close enough

to groom a baboon

Please don't try

to groom a baboon

we'll end up at your funeral

way too soon

you'll be torn to shreds

and your limbs will be strewn

so please, I beg you

Don't groom a baboon

Delaware Drifter

Leaning against the railings
taking it all in
the sights of Philadelphia
with this bottle and the skin I'm in

Twenty years or more ago
this scene would have seemed so remote
away on the company's dollar
on the Delaware
on this boat

I guess I could pinch myself
but I'm comfy now in beer
part of me still won't believe
that it's really me that's here

Amongst these special people
who seem to live for their work
evangelical souls
who've not sussed I'm a jerk

just some dodgy geezer

from a rotting seaside town

who somehow cleaned up his act enough

to earn himself a gown

Letters after the name

thought I'd feel different

but I still feel the same

a chancer, a dancer

an unworthy fool

a puller of wool over eyes to seem cool

they sucked it all up

the poison as well

I mean them no harm

but time, as always, will tell

Out on a limb

bluffing my way

now my hair is dappled

with clusters of grey

a life course changed

by two good decisions

when everyone thought I'd be dead

or in prison

but still I persist

doing just enough

and saying the right things

truism or bluff

and ten years later

I'm still holding on

to a job, not career

and it's *still* not gone wrong!

Soaking up the skyline

golden rays on my cheeks

this Delaware drifter

is not what he seems

August Bank Holiday Reggae has become quite a regular event (a hiatus during covid lockdown, naturally). Poster by James Domestic.

Soul DJing with partner, Lu. Poster by James Domestic.

The Whole Plane Thinks I'm in the Wrong

I lurch forward

spilling some of my overpriced rum 'n' coke

turbulence?

nah, I don't think so

a dreadful anti-rhythm

thumping

bashing

from behind

if I could work out the timing

maybe I could tip fore and aft

in some kind of syncopated style

y'know, like Gene Krupa

or Sly and Robbie

and spare myself the worst

but those guilty feet

have got no rhythm

so, it's a fruitless task

I accept, after a few minutes

that even the most 'out there'

prog-jazz-fusion drummer

couldn't lock in with this shit

what a bummer

It's like a band in a rehearsal room

when the guitarist is trying to tune up

and the drummer

either oblivious or uncaring

absent-mindedly

whacks the bejesus out of their kit

the guitarist takes a deep breath

and readies himself for a lull

so that he might finish

this simplest of tasks

D string

G string

B...

WHACK!

CRASH!

SMASH!

And that's what this flight's like

the reprieves are no reprieve at all

as I spend them braced

for the barrage to come

twitching and jerking

all the way to Montreal

I'm not comparing it *directly*

to the trenches of WWII

but...well, it is kind of like that

but without the sacrifice

without the blood and death

but the wait, the dread

the frayed nerves

the *knowing-it's-coming*

but-not-quite-when

of it must be similar

of course, I may be overstretching

pumping up my plight

on this mentally draining horror flight

but it's an eight hour haul

and I'm three hours in

and already I'm so far out of my mind

I fear I may never get back in

A tattoo of dull thuds

greet my fearful spine

I've tried twisting in my seat

peering over the headrest

like one of those Chad things

(sometimes called "wot no?'s")

that kids used to draw

in the seventies and eighties

and appealing to the parents

of this snotty demon-child

a number of times now

first verbally: a polite request

then with a *he's still doing it*

expression ten minutes later

my facial expressions

must be looking more desparate

and deranged each time

as I gradually slip my gentlemanly tether

and begin to seethe

I whirl around, dervish-like

unable to contain myself

I've been more than patient

but I need respite

but before I can spew forth

my rabid, but entirely justified, invective

I stop

both parents have vacated their seats

leaving this malfunctioning drum machine

of a child to its own devices

they're sick of the little shit too!

I don't blame them!

I'd be sick of him!

I *am* sick of him!

Hang on though

annoying as he is

he's just a kid

it's the parents who're to blame

and they've fucked off up the isle

to talk to another couple

maybe they know them

or maybe they're so exhausted

by their awful spawn

that they'll talk to almost anyone

as long as the payoff is a little distancing

between them and the boy

if only for a few minutes

The kid

I'm guessing he's about four or five

but I'm no good with ages

flashes a gappy grin at me

and boots the back of my seat again

and to think I was feeling a little sympathy!

Good God!

it's a Herculean effort

not to explode

but I don't

I close my eyes

take a few deep breaths

open them again and ask

in the calmest, most exacting

and serene voice I can muster

"Do you think you could stop doing that, please?

It's very annoying, and quite painful.

It'd make me very happy if you'd stop"

It was difficult work, I can tell you

I *wanted* to bawl him into next week

but I knew that

a) It's not my place, and
b) He's just a kid

so the calm and rational, saintly approach

is what he gets

I should win some sort of prize

for reigning that fury in!

Then the little fucker starts up again

this time screeching and crying

and making a right old din

took me by surprise

I'd done nothing wrong

I was nice and gentle

and made what I thought was a nice

and wholly sympathetic face

and now I'm frazzled with frustration

I'm dotty with despair

I've never felt so low

When I've been so high in the air

A stewardess trots down the isle

and as I'm marvelling

as I always do

at how they can look so pristine

even after an hour or two

I am confronted unexpectedly

and recoil from my interrogator

"What have you done to this child, sir

to create this situation?"

the parents appear

and both pile on

now the whole plane

thinks that I'm in the wrong!

"But he was kicking and thumping..."

I try to explain

"I asked him to stop and he did it again!"

and again, and again

The parents offer exaggerated tutts

the attendant looks stern

"you don't have kids, do you? Your sort never learn!"

and so it goes on

in a similar vein

my name is besmirched

my character stained

for a good ten minutes

and maybe some more
I'm dragging it out
and I'll tell you what for:
it's 'cos every minute of this
is a small victory
the kid's playing angel
good as gold in his seat
and my coccyx are smilin'
at this minor reprieve
my vertebrae joyful
like a sailor on leave
but it can't last forever
my diversionary scheme
soon for this rest
I'll undoubtedly grieve
the battery will commence
and I'll shake like a leaf
praying that this plane
will plunge into the sea

Scamps

I used to go to pubs

Full of hard scamps on smart E's

Now I got to pubs

With soft scampi and hard peas

About the author

James Domestic grew up in Essex, is a compulsive songwriter, a musician, soul and reggae DJ, poet, painter, and punk. He holds a doctorate from the University of Essex, has toured the world and elsewhere with *The Domestics*, and made records with more bands than is healthy or sensible. He resides in Suffolk with his partner, *Lucy*, and their two cats, *Freddie Fuzzles* and *Susan the Cat* and since *Vol.1* is under doctor's orders to drastically change his lifestyle lest his heart should go 'POP!' in a loud and catastrophic way.

Not sure when this was taken, or by whom, but it must have been pre-2007, as I'm lighting up. Although I'd stopped smoking cigarettes by this point – I'd gradually become a 40-a-day man – I would still occasionally enjoy a cigar in a pub (The Marquis of Granby, but always known simply as 'The Marquis', on North Hill, Colchester). Can't even stand cigars now...how times change!

Selected Discography

The Domestics: East Anglian Hardcore LP/CD (2023)

The Domestics: *Routine and Ritual* LP/CD (2014)

The Domestics: *Brutal Regimes* 7" E.P. (2016)

The Domestics: *Cherry Blossom Life* LP (2017)

The Domestics: *Pissing on Perfection* 7" E.P. (2017)

The Domestics: *Live in Oslo* LP (2018)

The Domestics/Pizzatramp: *Discipline* 5" E.P. (2018)

The Domestics/Wolfhour: "split" 7" E.P. (2019)

The Domestics/Pizzatramp: *No Life/This is Your Life* 12" (2020)

The Domestics: *A Gift to Your Masters* 7" E.P. (2020)

James Domestic: *Carrion Repeating* LP (2022)

Bring The Drones: *Ignorance Paradise* LP (2017)

PI$$ER: *Wretched Life* 7" E.P. (2019)

PI$$ER: *Crushed Down to Paste* 12" MLP (2020)

PI$$ER: *Carved Up for Yuks* 12" MLP (2021)

Botched Toe: *A False Glimmer of Hope* LP (2022)

Hazard Profile: *Slime* 7" E.P. (2021)

Körd Värld: *Total Distortion* 7" E.P. (2021)

Tokyo Lungs: *Tokyo Lungs* 7" E.P. (2020)

Tokyo Lungs: *Soul Music* LP (2021)

Tokyo Lungs/Feral State "split" 7" E.P. (2022)

Da Groins: *100% Groin* 7" E.P. (2022)

Domestic Curse: *The Five Curses* 12" MLP (2022)

Resources / Contact

For live dates, books, records, CDs, t shirts, paintings etc., visit: *www.jamesdomestic.com*. You can join the mailing list for occasional exclusives.

To book The Domestics (band), or James Domestic for a spoken word show, please email: *kibourecords@hotmail.co.uk*

You can find James Domestic on Facebook, Twitter, and Instagram (oh, and Tik Tok, but he doesn't really use it much)

Also available

Domesticated Vol.1
(Earth Island Books)

Cruor w/Dave Cullern
(Self-Published)

"Domestic's style is honed to perfection"
(Steven Midwinter, Personal Punk)

"Through his use of clever wordplay and satire, Domestic effortlessly dissects societal norms, political landscapes, and personal dilemmas. His ability to blend criticism with humour creates a refreshing and accessible reading experience, making the book intellectually stimulating and entertaining."
(Thoughts Words Action)

"His humour is voracious in his work but it can be as cutting as it is lively, or deeply poignant and emotionally impacting"
(Pete Ring, The Ringmaster Review)

"Eschewing obscurity, he writes in a bright and at times even colloquial tone, like a mate regaling stories down the pub... provoking laughter between lines of despair."
(Lee Taylor, The Screever)

"Very raw, very real, very deep"
(Matt Mackay, BBC Essex)

Milton Keynes UK
Ingram Content Group UK Ltd.
UKHW021450240124
436600UK00010B/70